Meditative Coloring
Book 5:

LABYRINTHS

Aliyah Schick

Sacred
Imprints

Other Books by Aliyah Schick

- *Mary Magdalene's Words: Two Women's Spiritual Journey, Both Truth and Fiction, Both Ancient and Now.*
- *Meditative Coloring Book 1: Angels*
- *Meditative Coloring Book 2: Crosses*
- *Meditative Coloring Book 3: Ancient Symbols*
- *Meditative Coloring Book 4: Hearts*
- *Finally, a Book of Poetry by Aliyah Schick*

Table of Contents

Dedicated to
peaceful moments,
open hearts,
and
self-discovery.

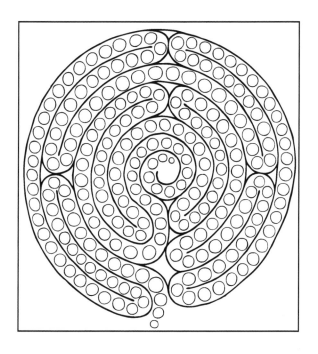

Walking a Labyrinth

Labyrinths are now being built or brought in to communities all across the country and the world. There may very possibly be one or more near where you live. You might walk a labyrinth at an community event or for a special occasion at a church, or visit a labyrinth at a college or retreat center. Walking a nearby labyrinth may become a favorite regular practice. You might even construct one in your own backyard.

This book, Labyrinths: Meditative Coloring Book 5, plus carved finger-walking labyrinths, quilted labyrinths, printed labyrinths, and many other portable options make it possible for you to "walk" a labyrinth wherever and whenever you want.

Walking a labyrinth, whether with your feet, coloring the path's steps, tracing with a pointer or a finger, or following it with your eyes, can change you. It has been called a pilgrimage, a spiritual journey, a path toward personal growth, enlightenment or salvation. It invites you to embrace your soul and come away with more of who you really are. Walking a labyrinth can change your life, expand what is possible, open intuition, vision, wisdom, healing, and strength.

One Path

Most labyrinths you will encounter are circular with one entrance at the outer edge, a single winding and turning path to the center, and the same path in reverse back out again. Since there are no choices along the way, no dead ends, and no tricks, your mind can relax and allow walking the labyrinth to become a deepening spiritual journey.

Meditative Mind

All those turns and twists and loops cause you to lose your sense of direction and familiar relationship with the outside world. Next thing you know, your mind gives up, releases, and becomes receptive. You're just on the path, walking the path, staying on the path, following the path. You're in that altered, meditative, prayerful state that opens you to higher understanding, purpose, answers, and healing.

Intention

Often the journey into the labyrinth is taken with a question in mind, or a prayer, or a need for healing. As you move further into the labyrinth, you descend deeper into willingness, into yourself, and into sacred wisdom. An answer or realization or healing change may come as you reach the center, or it may come on your way back out to rejoin ordinary life. Or perhaps later, whenever you are ready to receive it.

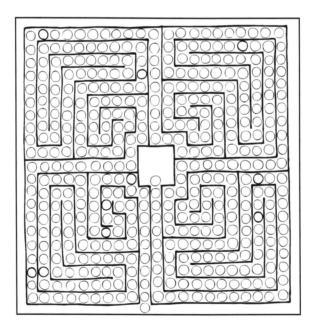

Rhythm

Different labyrinths have different rhythmic patterns, like songs. The shorter runs of inner circuits and the quick turns in complex designs create a faster rhythm with higher energy. Long, unbroken sections in simple designs or in the outer circuits relax and ease the experience. Whether you color it, walk it, trace with your finger or pointer, or just follow the path with your eyes, you absorb the rhythm and feel its effects.

One labyrinth's design may take you quickly into the inner circles where circuits are short and quick, increasing the energy and gathering your attention. From there it may then slow you down out in the long, extended outer circuits. Another labyrinth may do the reverse, building slowly from wide, leisurely outer circuits to the faster, compelling turns toward the center.

The simplest forms of labyrinth have fewer turns and may take you nearly all the way around the circle before reversing direction. More complex designs turn much more often, suddenly sending you this way and that. Differences in these design patterns create a rhythm specific to each labyrinth, and a different experience for you when you walk it.

One advantage of the collection of varied labyrinth drawings in Labyrinths: Meditative Coloring Book 5 is that you get to choose which labyrinth you want to walk today. See which one catches your attention, which one draws you in, which one feels right. Whichever labyrinth you choose, all lead to your inner, true self where wisdom, guidance, and spiritual connection await.

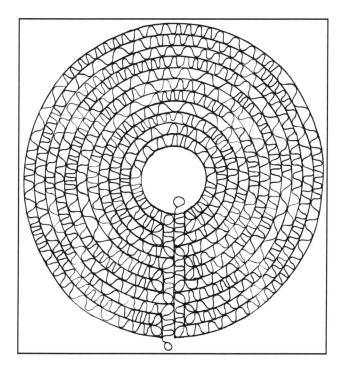

Respite

Walking a labyrinth with colored markers, feet, fingers, or eyes provides welcome respite from our busy, commercial, fast-paced, overloaded lives. It brings us into balance, calm, intuitive wisdom, spiritual connection, and peace, where we can access the best of ourselves and learn to be more of what we are meant to be.

Basic Labyrinth Forms

The Oldest Labyrinths

The oldest and simplest labyrinth patterns are called "Classical." Earliest known examples are Neolithic and early Bronze Age petroglyphs carved into natural stone in sacred sites and underground burial chambers. They are usually drawn building from two crossed lines. Iron Age turf labyrinths (500 to 0 BCE) in southern Sweden are the oldest identified for walking.

3 Circuit Classical Labyrinth

7 Circuit Classical Labyrinth

[Note: Learn how to draw these two classical labyrinths on page 8.]

The Roman Labyrinths

The Romans mainly used labyrinth designs as decorative floor mosaics, not for walking. Theirs were more complex patterns, including squares, spirals, repeating quadrants, and labyrinths within labyrinths.

Sample Roman Labyrinth, Beginning of 3rd Century C.E.

Medieval Labyrinths: Chartres

Medieval labyrinths flourished in manuscript illustrations beginning in the 9th century. Labyrinth designs were installed as floor decorations in Medieval Italian churches and cathedrals in the early 12th century.

Several large floor labyrinths for walking were built in France in the early 13th century. The Chartres Cathedral's famous labyrinth is the only one of these remaining. The Chartres labyrinth has roots in a 12th century Otfrid manuscript labyrinth that expanded Medieval designs to 11 circuits.

Medieval Otfrid Manuscript Labyrinth
12th Century

Chartres Cathedral Labyrinth
Early 13th Century

Modern Day Labyrinths

Labyrinths are now being built at churches, schools, hospitals, parks, companies, community sites, and private property. These labyrinths serve meditation, personal growth, healing, community building, and ceremony. Most of these new labyrinths use either the simple classical designs or the Chartres' medieval formality. Some explore innovative design, pushing the labyrinth's creative limits, transforming sacred geometry into modern works of art to be experienced as well as viewed.

How to Draw a Classical 3-Circuit Labyrinth

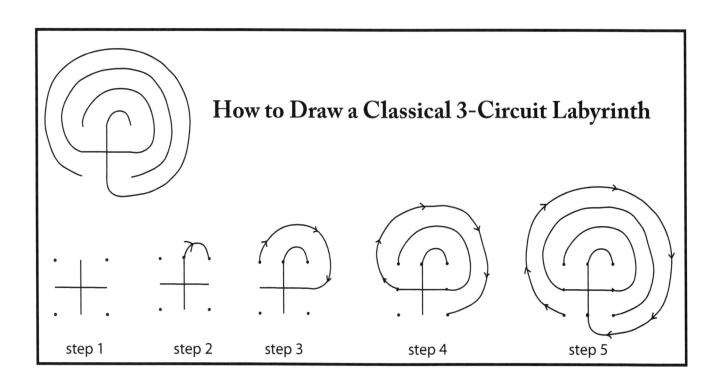

step 1   step 2   step 3   step 4   step 5

How to Draw a Classical 7-Circuit Labyrinth

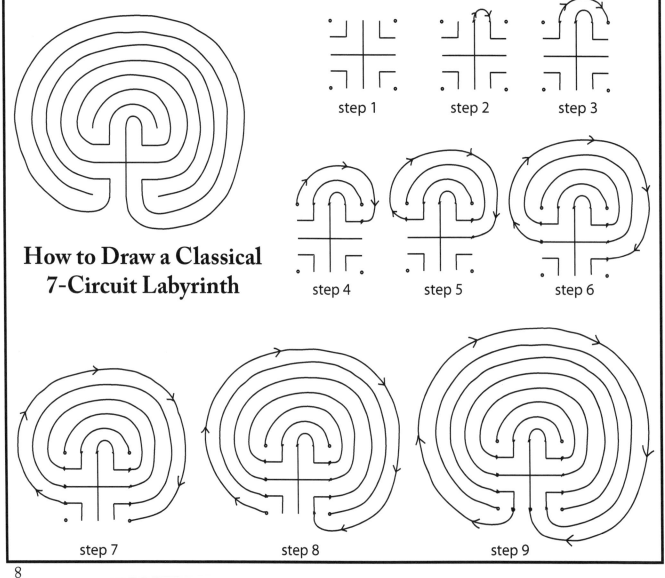

step 1   step 2   step 3

step 4   step 5   step 6

step 7   step 8   step 9

Labyrinth Resources

Labyrinth Society (http://labyrinthsociety.org)
An international organization to support those who create, maintain and use labyrinths. Use their online Labyrinth Locator to find a labyrinth near you.

Bibliography (www.labyrinth-enterprises.com/bibliography.html)
An extensive bibliography of labyrinth books.

Labyrinth Company (www.labyrinthcompany.com)
A source for do-it-yourself labyrinth kits printed on weed-blocking landscape fabric and stencils for use with pavers, bricks, or concrete.

Caerdroia: The Journal of Mazes and Labyrinths (www.labyrinthos.net)
Features articles from labyrinth aficianados. Published continuously for more than 20 years.

Labyrinth Books

Walking a Sacred Path: Rediscovering the Labyrinth as a Spiritual Practice, by Rev. Dr. Lauren Artress

The Sacred Path Companion: A Guide to Walking the Labyrinth to Heal and Transform, by Rev. Dr. Lauren Artress

Labyrinths for the Spirit: How to Create Your Own Labyrinths for Meditation and Enlightenment, by Jim Buchanan

Labyrinths from the Outside In: Walking to Spiritual Insight, A Beginner's Guide, by Donna Schaper and Carole A. Camp

Living the Labyrinth: 101 Paths to a Deep Connection to the Sacred, by Jill Geoffrion

Constructing Classical Labyrinths, by Robert Ferre

The Way of the Labyrinth: A Powerful Meditation for Everyday Life, by Helen Post Curry

Labyrinths for Kids, by Lani Rossetta

Rocklady: The Building of a Labyrinth, by Narah Griggs

Suggestions for How to Use This Book

Use this *Sacred Imprints*^{TM} *Meditative Coloring Book* for spiritual connection, prayer, relaxation, healing, centering, and for coming into your deep, true self. You may simply wish to experience the images in quiet contemplation. Or, you may focus on a prayer or affirmation as you work with colors. You may ask for understanding regarding an issue you are dealing with. You may ask for a clearer sense of some aspect of yourself and how it serves you. You may wish to learn about your path or purpose in this lifetime.

Open your heart and your mind as you use this *Sacred Imprints*^{TM} *Meditative Coloring Book*. Pay attention to impressions and ideas, feelings, intuition, and messages. They may very well be exactly what you need to hear.

Tools
Choose your favorite coloring tools, or you might like to gather a variety of pens, crayons, colored pencils, chalk, oil pastels, markers, glitter pens, paints, etc. You may want to place a blank sheet of paper behind the page so ink or paint does not go through.

Music
Consider playing soft instrumental or contemplative background music.

Nature
Sometimes a favorite spot outdoors provides just the right environment for creative expression. Beach, woods, backyard, porch, treehouse, mountain top, stream, pond, park, etc.

Silence
You may prefer quiet, so that all your attention focuses on what you are doing. Emptiness can give rise to profound experience.

Meditation
You may like to meditate first, and then begin working with the colors. Try any of the many ways of meditation, or simply be with your breath for a few minutes, following it in and out. Or, you may wish to try the following meditation. Read it silently or out loud, slowly, pausing to draw in each breath.

Meditation

Take in a breath... and on the exhale release the day's happenings, settling into this peaceful time of creative, spiritual connection.

Take in a breath... and on the exhale let go of worries and troubles and burdens. You can pick them up again later if you need to.

Take in a breath... and on the exhale come into the center of your Self. From there drop a line down through your body, through the chair and the floor and into the earth. Through soil and sand and stone, through coal and underground stream, and minerals and precious metals. Down through all the colors and textures and densities of the earth, down into the hot magma at this planet's core. Down to the very center of the earth, to the Heart of the Mother. Tie your line there. Anchor yourself there.

Take in a breath... and on the exhale extend your line up from your center, through your body and out the crown of your head, up through the ceiling, the roof, and into the sky. Past clouds and wind and thinning gases, out through the atmosphere and into space. Past the sun and galaxy and stars and universe, out to the depths of the Source of All That Is. Feel your connection there. You are part of the great cosmos. You are one with all being.

Take in a breath... and on the exhale return to the drawing before you and ask that you be open to receiving guidance and understanding as you spend time with it. Know that there are no mistakes, only new choices and combinations and patterns that suggest new perception at an other-than-conscious level. Or that remind us of something that can now be released. Or that create an opening to new possibilities.

Take in a breath... and on the exhale release "shoulds" and rules and expectations. Let go and open to new possibilities.

Now, begin by picking up whatever color catches your attention.

About the Artist

Aliyah Schick has been an artist all of her life. After Peace Corps in the Andes Mountains of South America, she studied art full time for four years, then created and sold pottery and ceramic art pieces for many years. Later Aliyah worked in fiber and fabric, making soft sculptural wall pieces and art quilts, then fabric dolls designed to carry healing energy. Now she draws and paints, and she writes poems and prose.

At the heart of all this, Aliyah's real work is healing. She is a skilled and dynamic deep energetic healer and Transformation Coach. Her work in the multidimensional layers and patterns of the auric field is powerful and effective. The **Sacred Imprints** ™ drawings, paintings, poetry, and writings, and the **Meditative Coloring** ™ **Books** emerged as new expressions of Aliyah's healing work. Experiencing these drawings serves to remind us who we are, where we come from, and why we are here.

Aliyah lives and works in the beautiful Blue Ridge Mountains of North Carolina, where the energy of the earth is easily accessible, ancient, motherly, and obvious. A place where people speak with familiarity and reverence of the land and spirit, and where the sacred comes to sit with us on the porch to share the afternoon sun.

www.AliyahSchick.com

The
Drawings

Opposite each drawing is a blank page labeled
Meditative Impressions. Use these pages to catch
and keep hold of your thoughts, wishes, intentions,
affirmations, prayers, poems, memories, notes,
drawings, or whatever comes to you as you explore
coloring with this book. Make it yours.

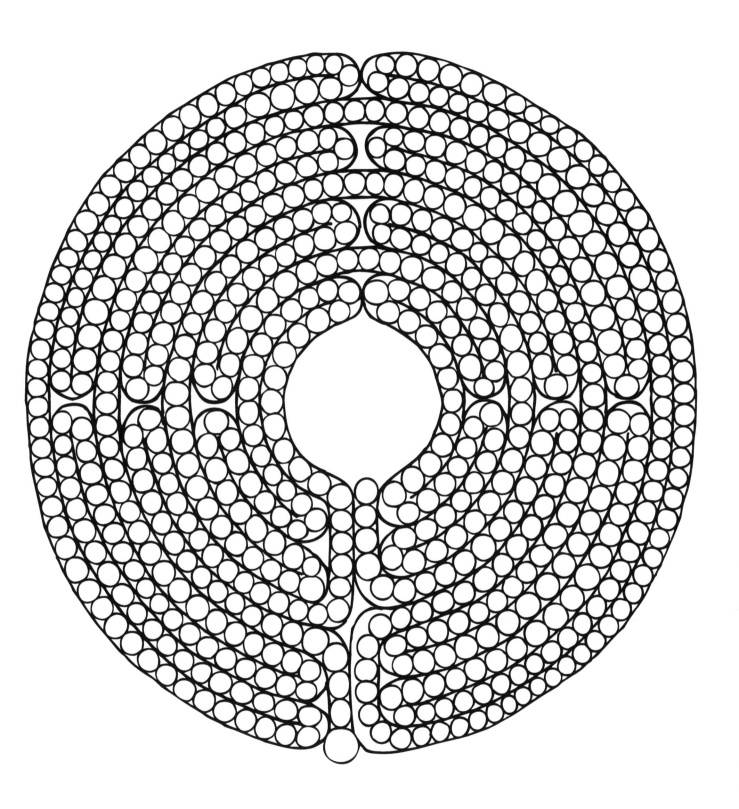

15

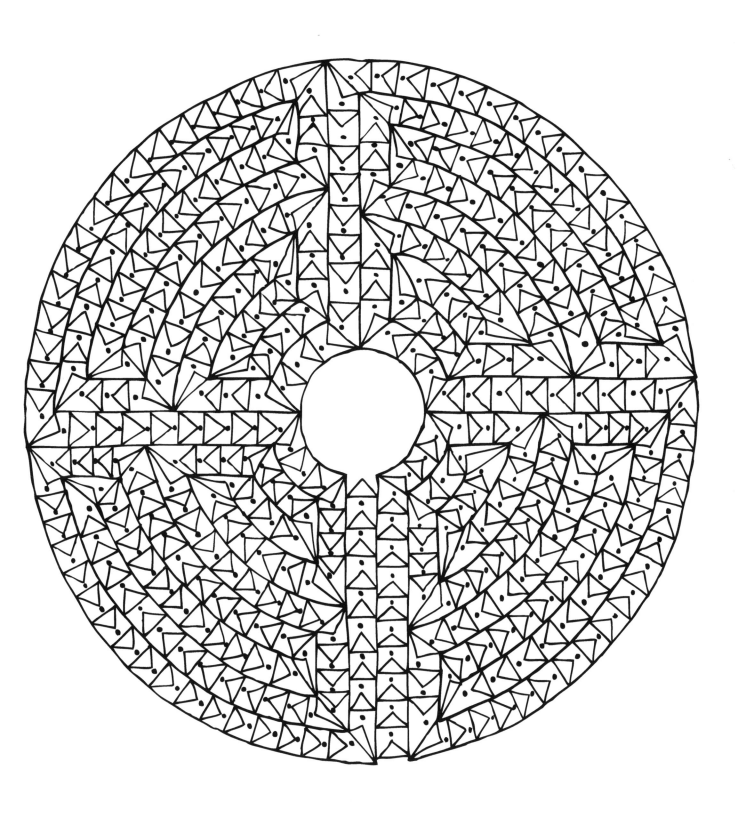

Meditative Impressions

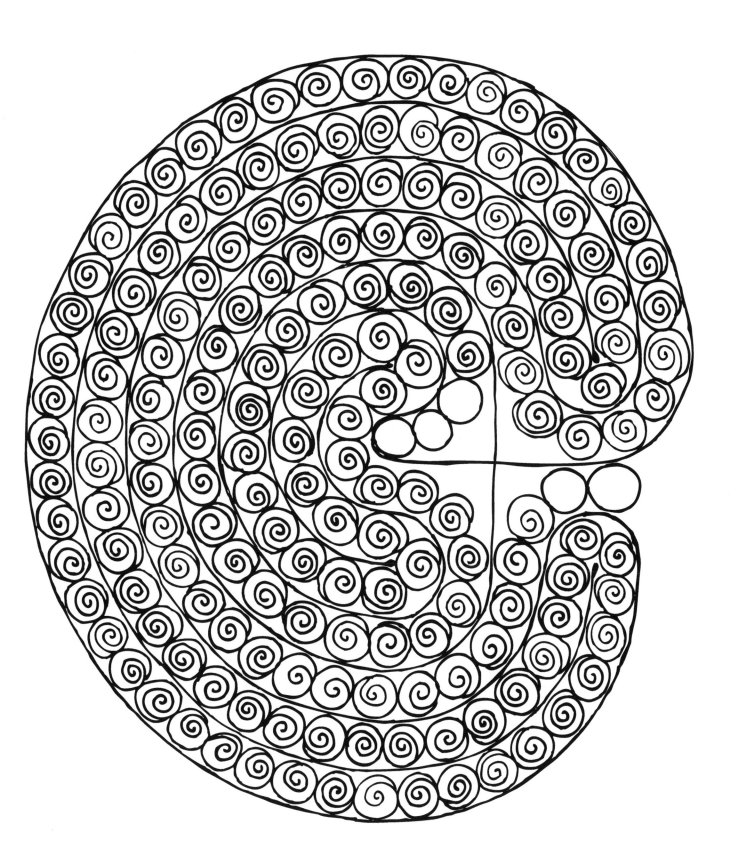

Meditative Impressions

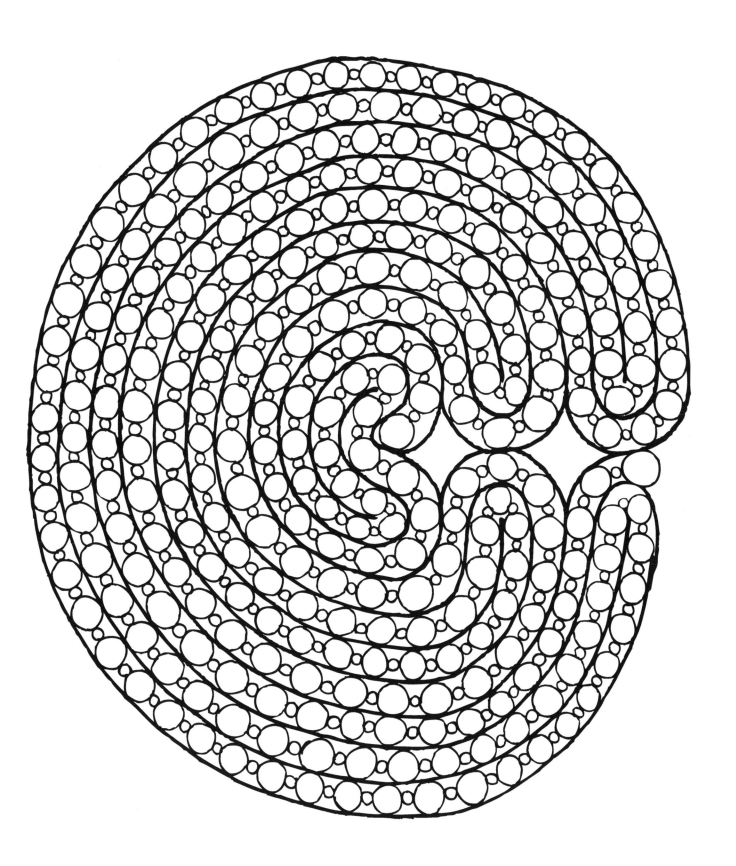

Meditative Impressions

Meditative Impressions

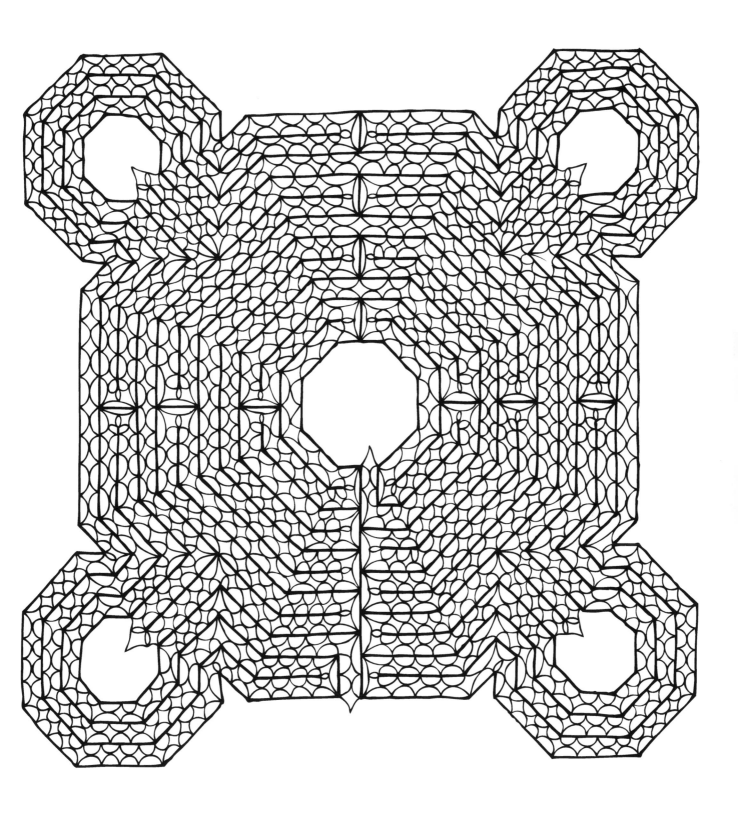

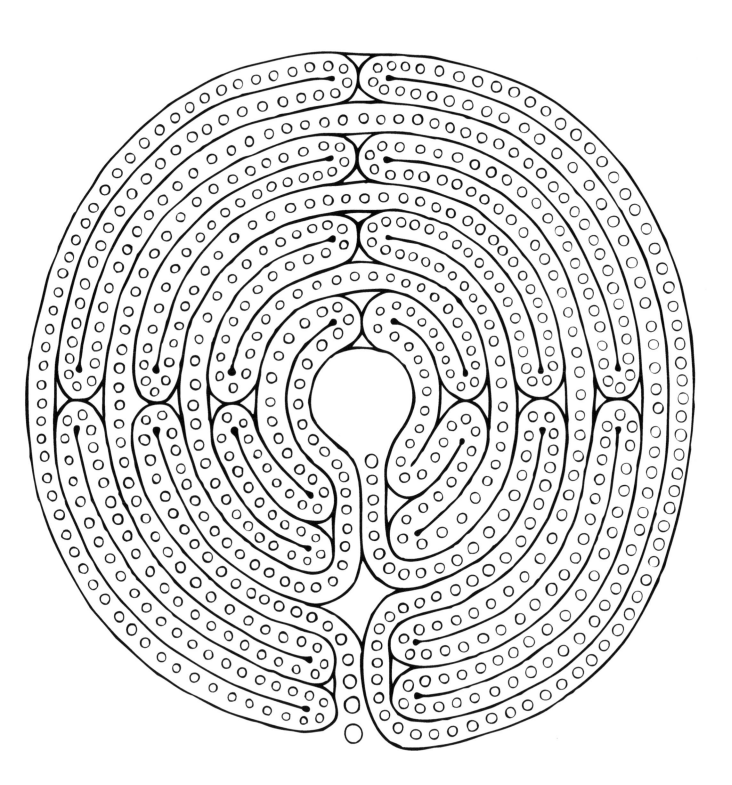

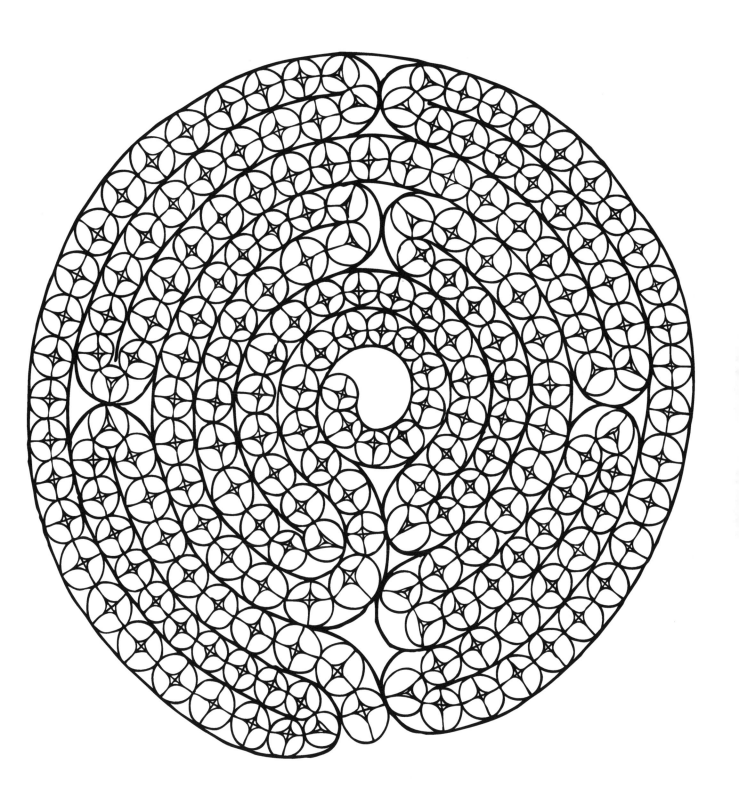

Meditative Impressions

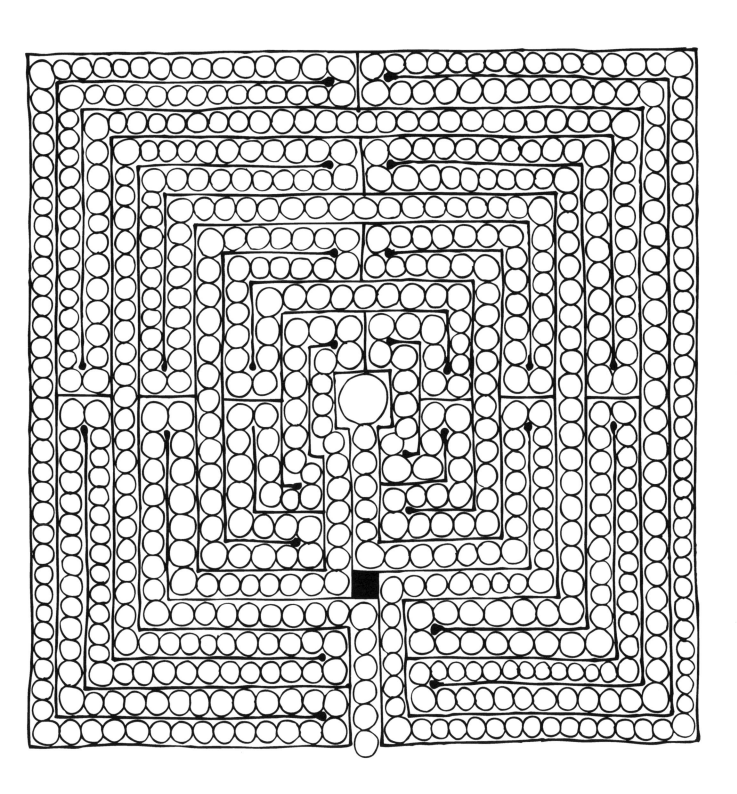

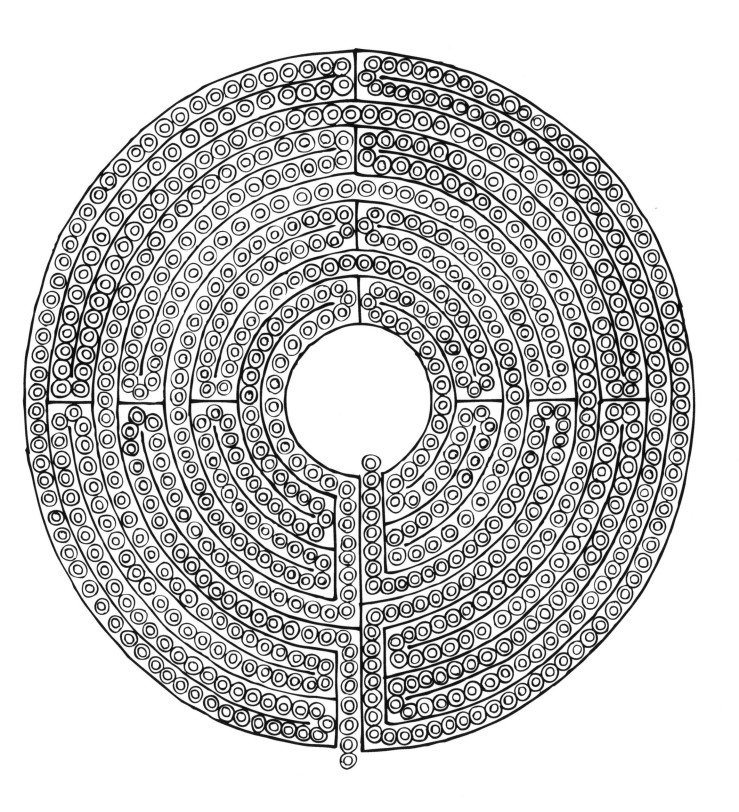

Meditative Impressions

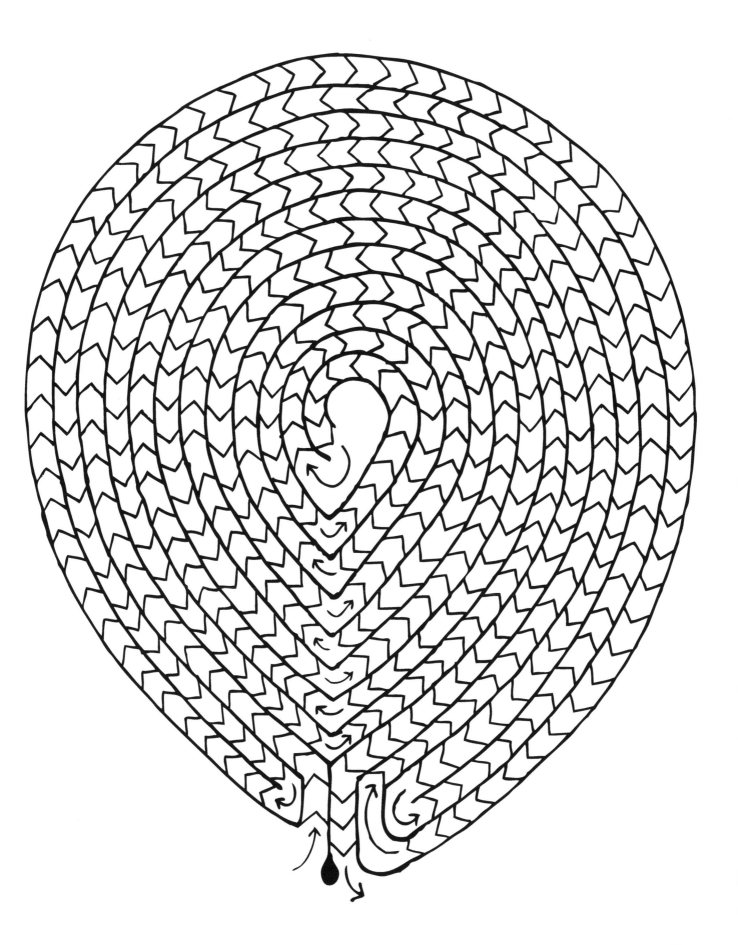

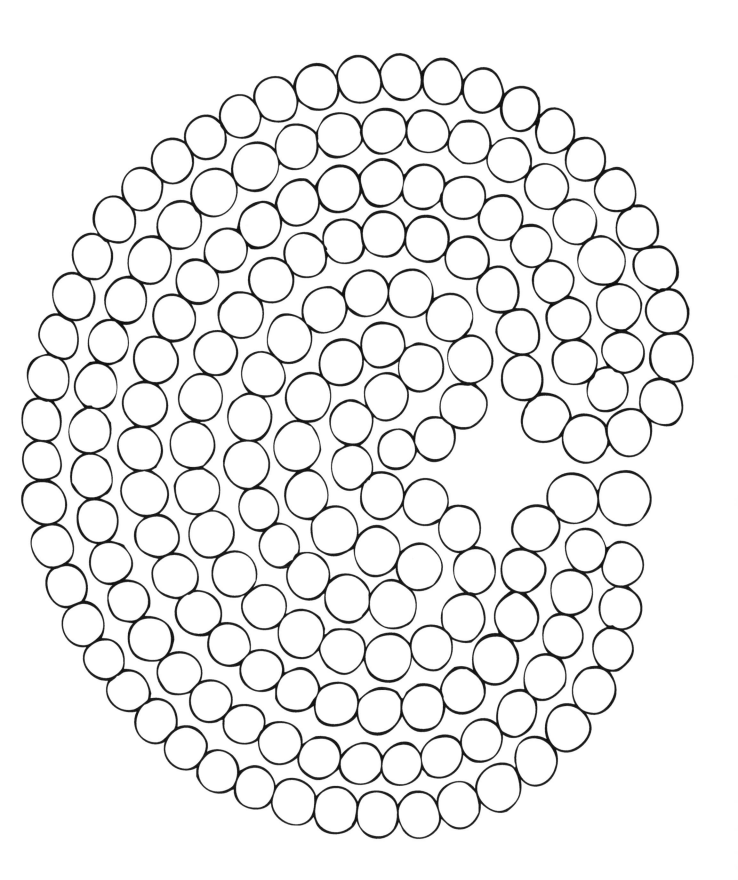

Meditative Impressions

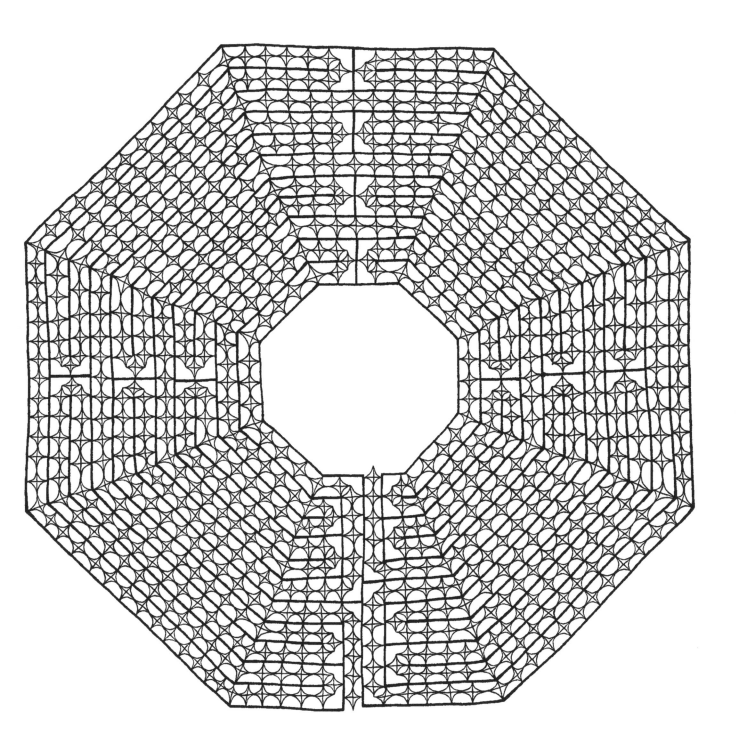

Meditative Impressions

Meditative Impressions

48

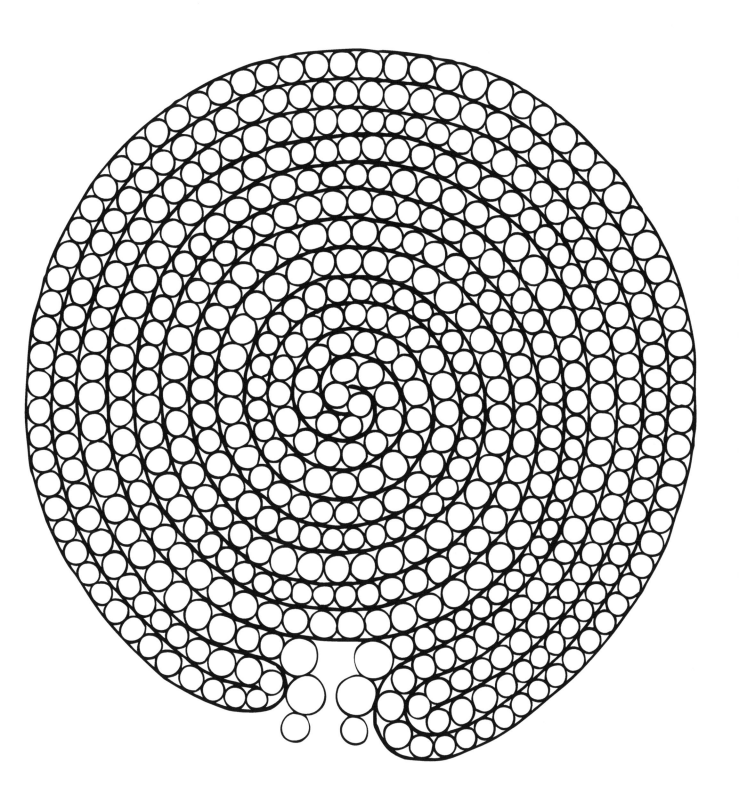

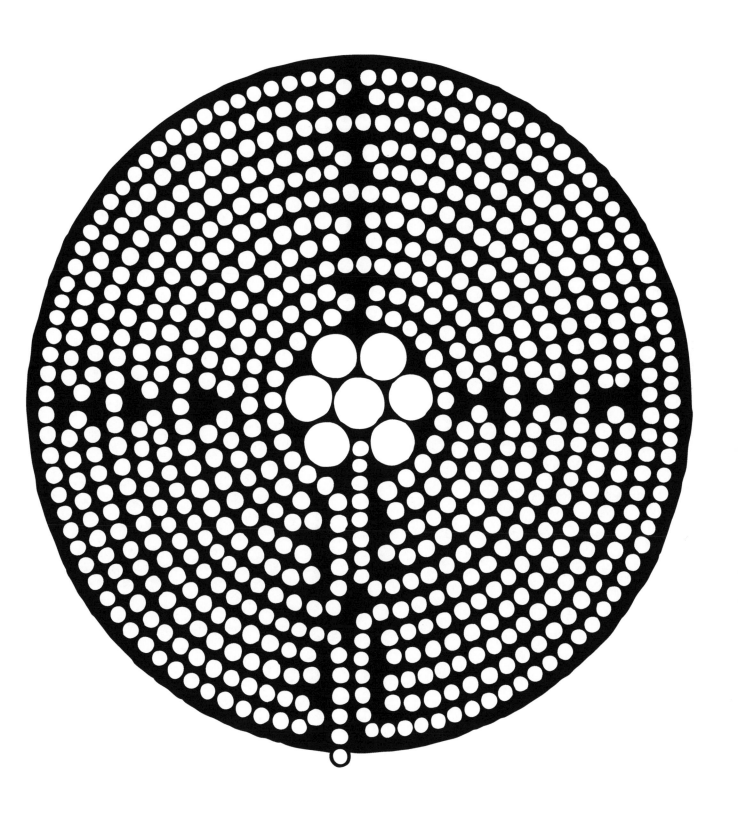

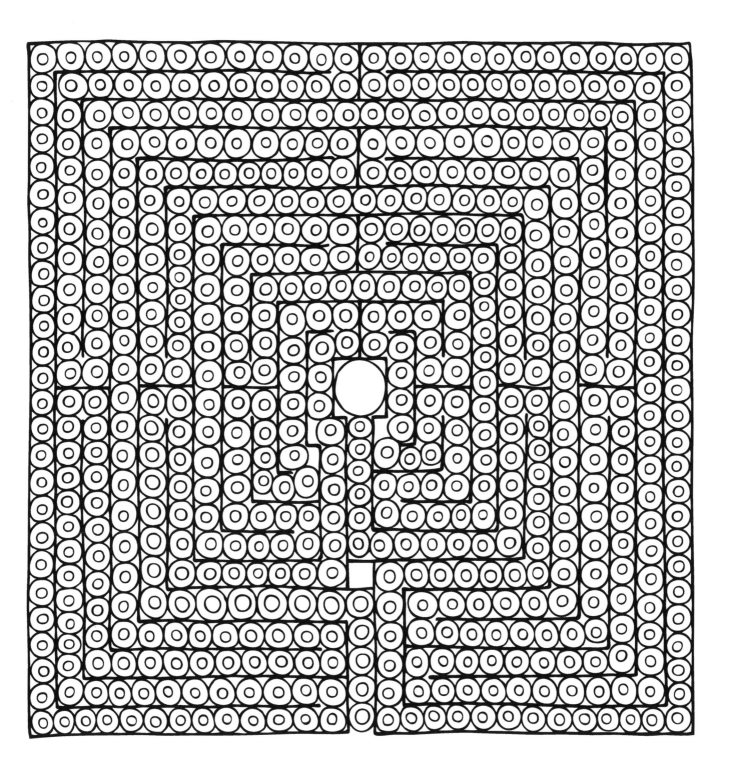

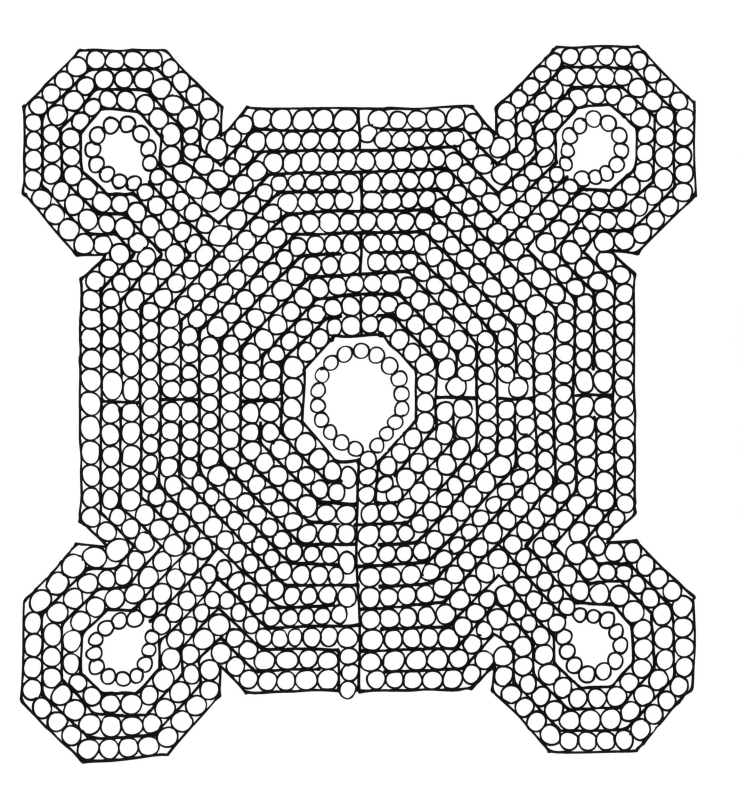

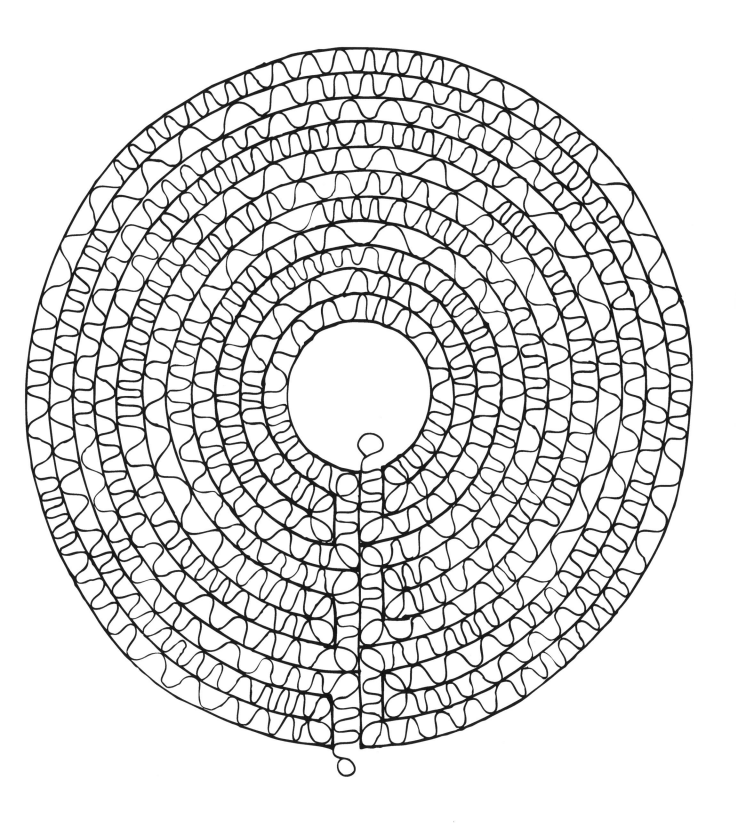

Meditative Impressions

62

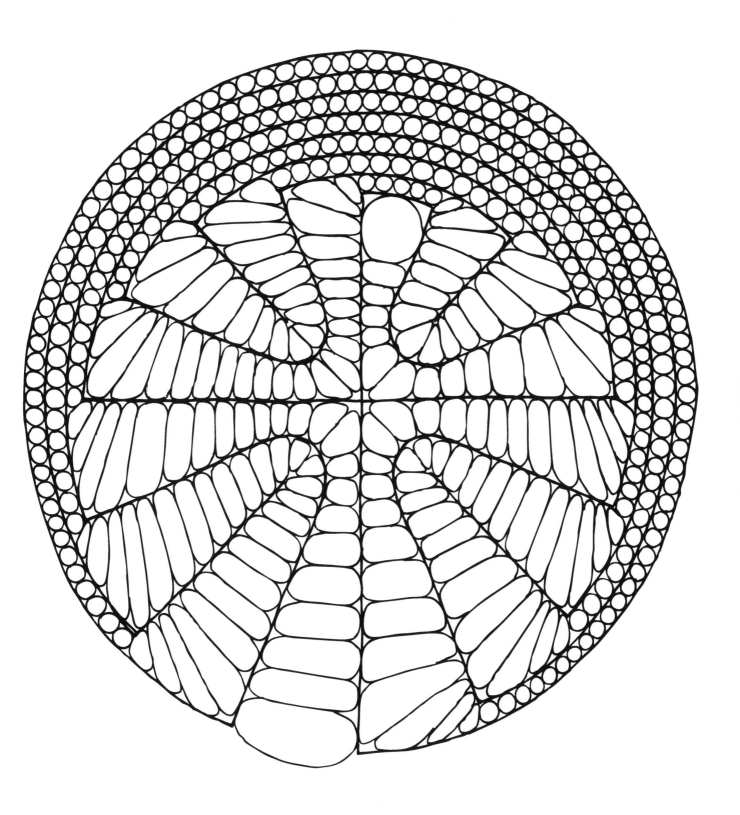

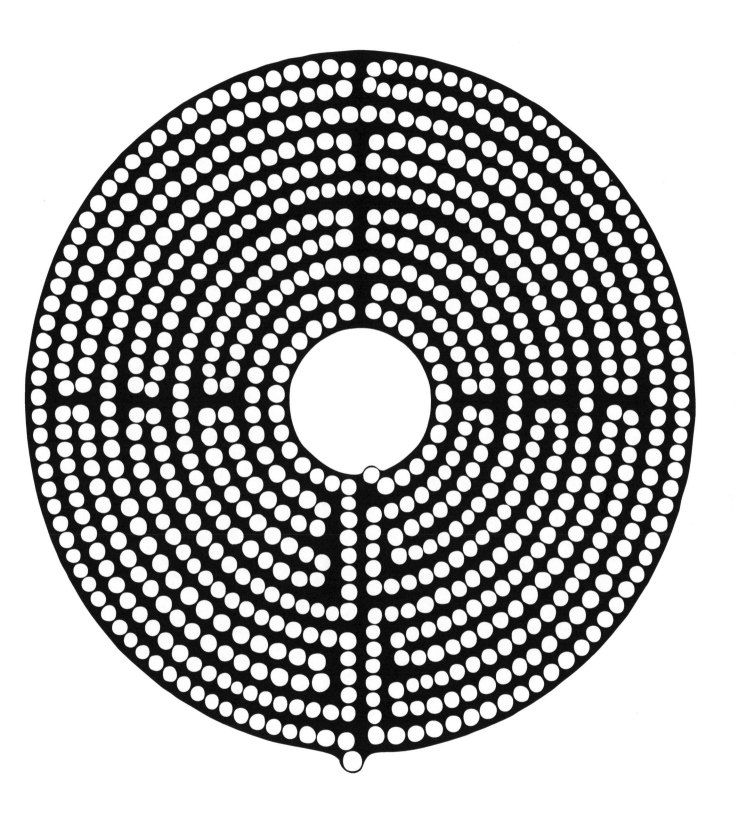

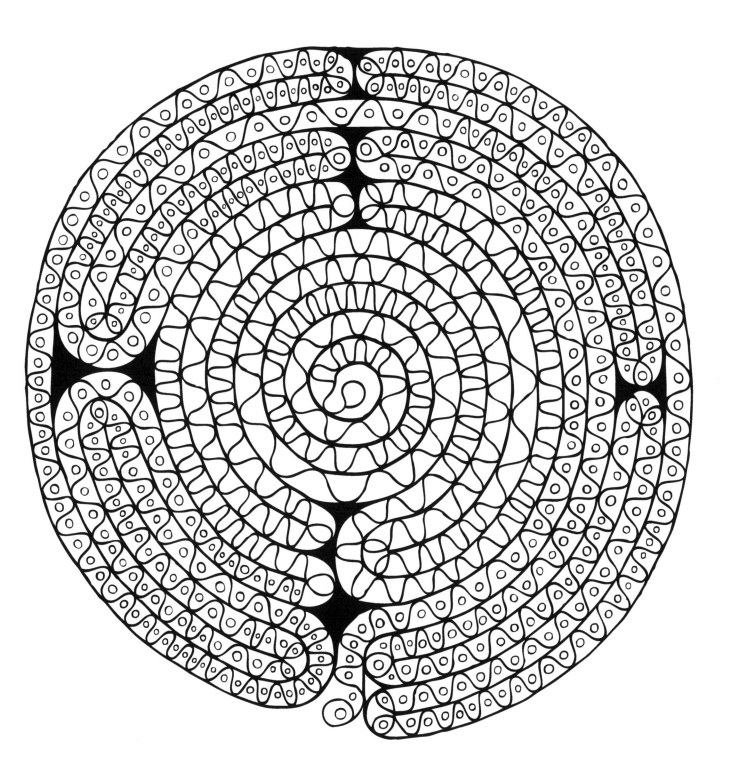

Meditative Impressions

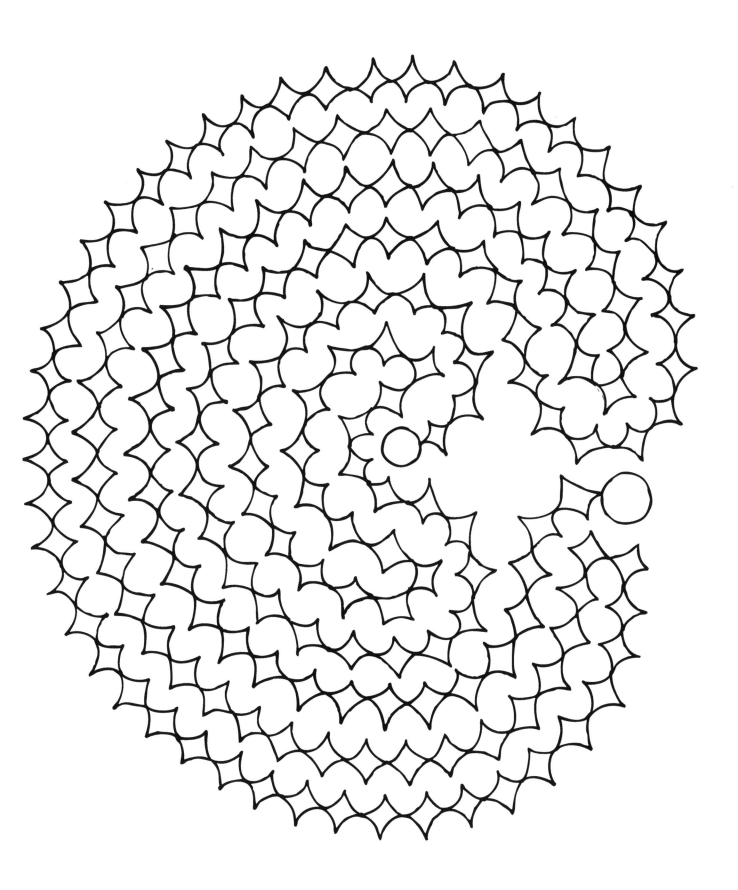

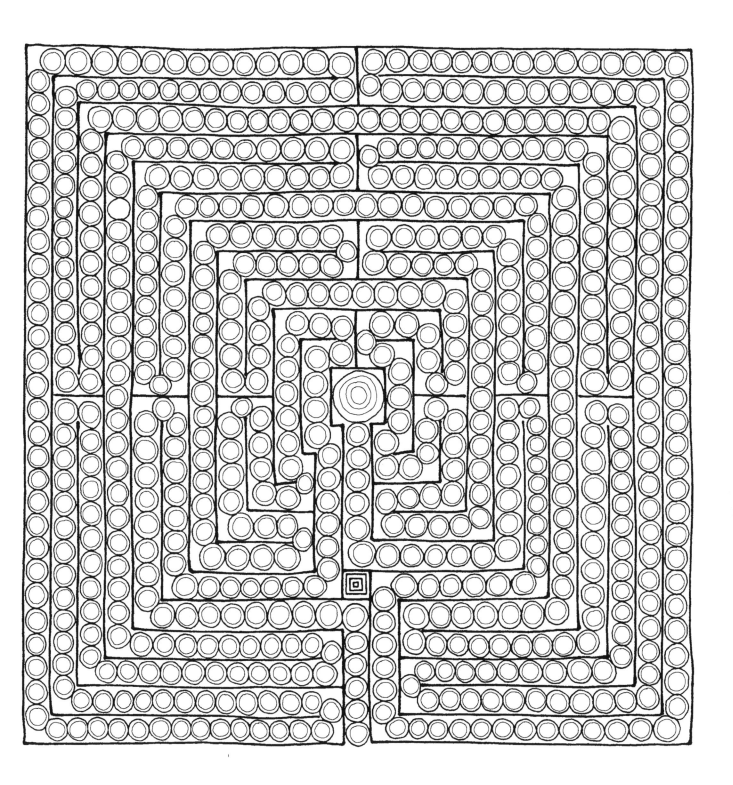

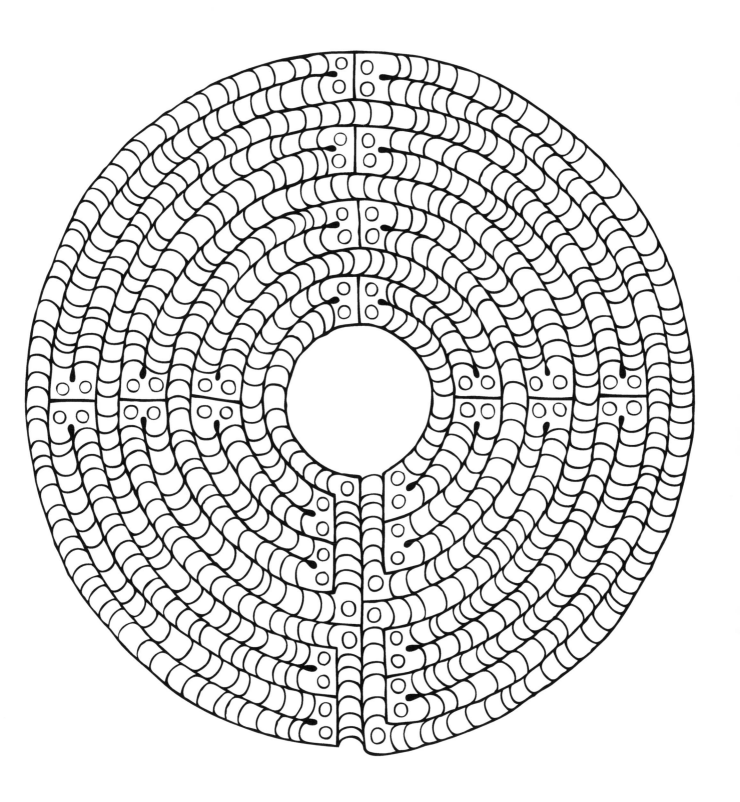

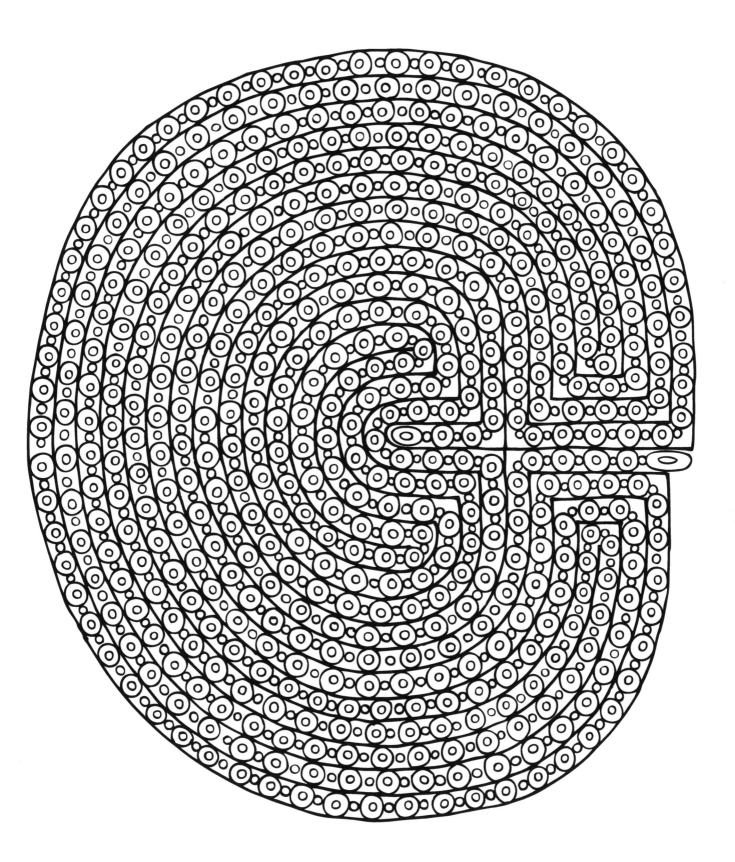

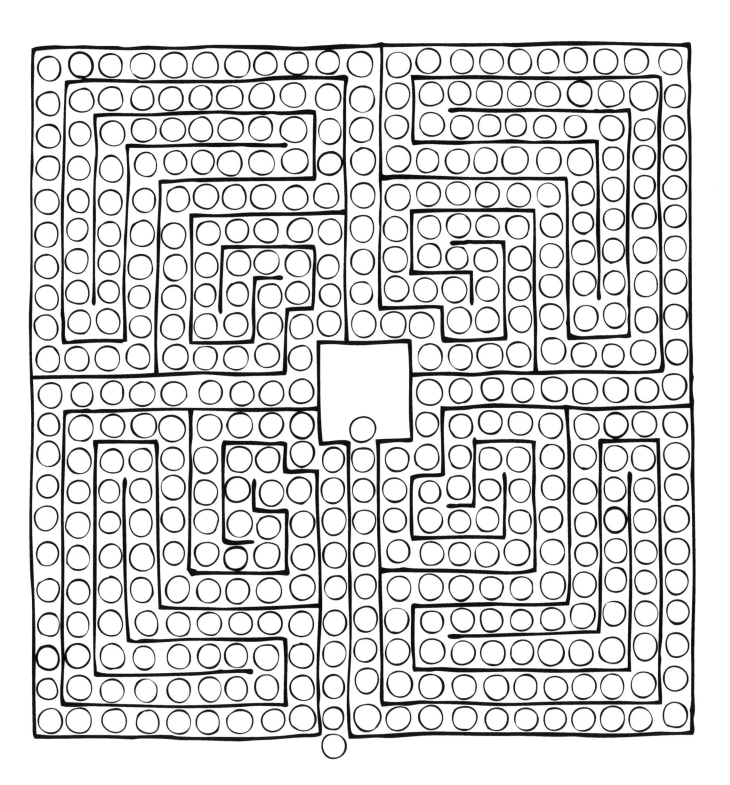

Meditative Impressions

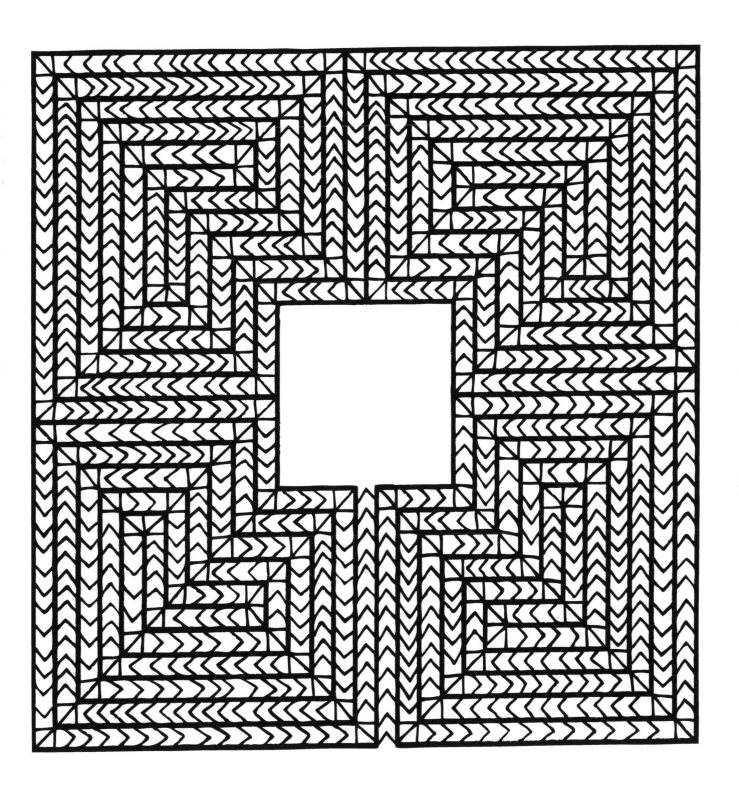

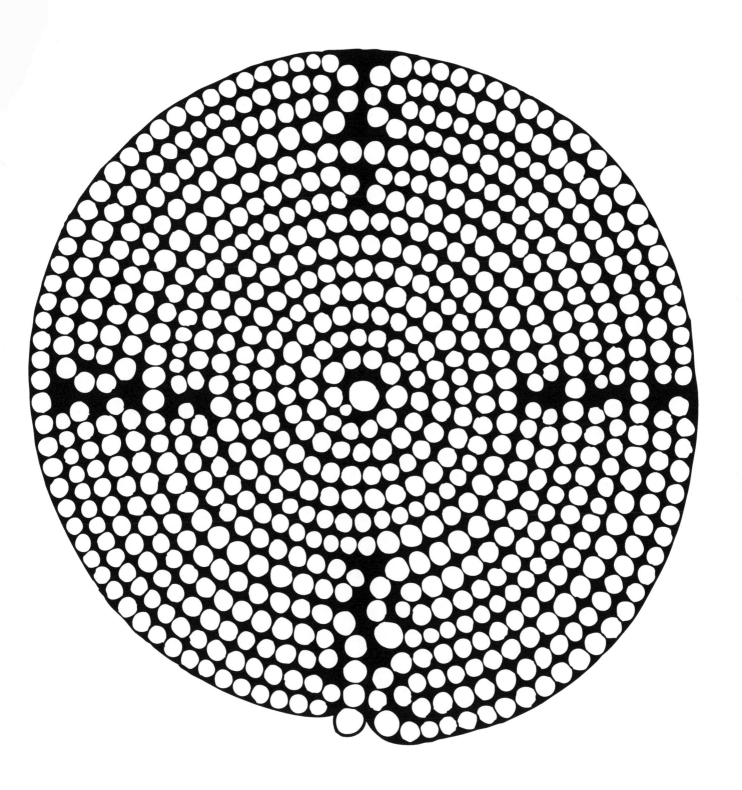

The Sacred Imprints™ Meditative Coloring Books
Five Volumes: Angels, Crosses, Ancient Symbols, Hearts, and Labyrinths

---

<u>Meditative Coloring Book 1 -- Angels</u>

The Sacred Imprints ™ Angelic images are drawn during a centering meditation. With a pen in each hand, Aliyah allows the lines to go where they will, the two sides mirroring each other. Every movement is guided by spirit; every drawing is different; and each one is a wonderful surprise filled with angelic presence.

<u>Meditative Coloring Book 2 -- Crosses</u>

The cross is one of our most ancient and enduring sacred symbols, found in nearly every culture throughout human existence. It symbolizes the celestial, spirtual divine coming into being in this material world. It represents God taking form, and the integration of soul into physical life. The drawings of the Crosses Series feature ancient and contemporary images of the cross in reflections of the deep spiritual significance of its form.

Meditative Coloring Book 3 -- Ancient Symbols

Ancient and indigenous sacred images speak deeply to us, to our bellies and our bones, to our cellular memory and our wisdom, to our souls' yearnings. Native peoples throughout time and place see the sacred in all of life. For them, holiness is life and life is holiness. Life is the manifestation of the holy in all things. The drawings of the Ancient Symbols Series feature timeless designs used by every culture on earth to remind us of the sacred.

Meditative Coloring Book 4 -- Hearts

The heart is one of our favorite symbols, evoking feelings of love, caring, loyalty, and devotion. As you spend time with these Sacred Imprints Heart drawings, open your heart to live with more compassion for others and for yourself. Open your life to deeper connection with the earth and all of life. Open yourself to recognize the sacred in all things, including in yourself.

Meditative Coloring Book 5 -- Labyrinths

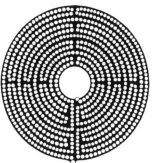

These original artist's labyrinth drawings invite you to color your steps into the labyrinth, one by one, as you contemplate, meditate, or pray. Go deep into your inner wisdom and guidance where questions' answers reveal themselves and choices come clear. Or simply relax and be with your breathing. Now you can bring your labyrinth with you to wherever you need to be.

Sacred
Imprints

12081554R00051

Made in the USA
Lexington, KY
21 November 2011